Learn German

Step by Step Guide For Learning The Basics of The German Language

Dave Smith

© **Copyright 2018 by Dave Smith**

All rights reserved.

The following eBook is reproduced below with the goal of providing information that is as accurate and reliable as possible. Regardless, purchasing this eBook can be seen as consent to the fact that both the publisher and the author of this book are in no way experts on the topics discussed within and that any recommendations or suggestions that are made herein are for entertainment purposes only. Professionals should be consulted as needed prior to undertaking any of the action endorsed herein.

This declaration is deemed fair and valid by both the American Bar Association and the Committee of Publishers Association and is legally binding throughout the United States.

Furthermore, the transmission, duplication or reproduction of any of the following work including specific information will be considered an illegal act irrespective of if it is done electronically or in print. This extends to creating a secondary or tertiary copy of the work or a recorded copy and is only allowed with an expressed written consent from the Publisher. All additional rights reserved.

The information in the following pages is broadly considered to be truthful and accurate account of facts, and as such any inattention, use or misuse of the information in question by the reader will render any resulting actions solely under their purview. There are no scenarios in which the publisher or the original author of this work can be in any fashion deemed liable for any hardship or damages that may befall them after undertaking information described herein.

Additionally, the information in the following pages is intended only for informational purposes and should thus be thought of as universal. As befitting its nature, it is presented without assurance regarding its prolonged validity or interim quality. Trademarks that are mentioned are done without written consent and can in no way be considered an endorsement from the trademark holder.

Table of Contents

Introduction 4
Chapter 1: What it means to learn German 5
Chapter 2: Finding your passion for learning German 16
Chapter 3: Immersing yourself in German culture 22
Chapter 4: Finding native speakers to increase your overall understanding of the language and culture 35
Chapter 5: How to beat the most difficult part of learning the German language 41
Chapter 6: Learning German in a more formal classroom environment 49
Conclusion 51

Introduction

Thank you and congratulations on downloading *Learn German*. The German language is the 11th most widely spoken language on earth with 92 to 95 million native speakers around the globe composing 1.39% of the world's population. By downloading this book, you are taking the first steps in your own personal conquest in learning this great and storied language. The following chapters will be more of a general outline on what steps to take when first learning the language and how to develop and apply the skills necessary to master German.

Here are some of the topics which will be discussed within this brief book:

- What it means to learn Standard German, High German, and Low German;
- Finding your passion for learning German;
- Turning a chore into inspiration;
- Learning German by immersing yourself deeply in the German culture;
- Finding native speakers to improve your overall understanding of the language and its culture;
- How to overcome the most difficult part of learning the German language; and finally
- Learning German in a more formal class environment.

These following chapters will, more precisely, discuss the study techniques applicable to learning a new language, the culture of Germany as well as the rest of German speaking Europe, some of the history of the language and its various dialects, steps for beginning the study of the language, and learning German inside and outside of formal class settings.

There are a number of books on the market very similar to this one. Thank you again for choosing this one and if you enjoy it or find it helpful, a review on Amazon would be very much appreciated.

Chapter 1:
What it means to learn German

Standard German, Low German, and High German

Learning German

Learning a foreign language is, to the inexperienced, one of intimidating tasks that education has to offer and, to the polyglot, one of the rewarding and advantageous tasks that education can make a person do. As with developing any new skill set, learning a language takes lots of time, effort, and practice, but once the brain starts to make the new connections necessary for progress and the learner starts to build confidence and skill, the transition from intermediate to fluent can be a lot smoother than the transition from beginner to intermediate. The learning curve can increase exponentially.

The contemporary world is more globalized and interconnected than it ever has been. This is a fact that extols the practicality of learning a second language. But the reasons for learning go beyond just geopolitics, they vary widely. We should now examine some of the innumerable benefits of learning a second language:

1. Connection
Multilingualism breaks down barriers that are very real to monolingual people. In learning a second language, there is constant opportunity to expand horizons and make connections with new people which would have been out of question beforehand.

2. Career Advancement
Multilingualism doubles as a major competitive advantage in virtually any line of work. Not only will it help you on getting hired, but it also statistically increases salary and benefits. As far as employment is concerned, there is no down side to learning a second language.

3. Cognitive Benefits
This is a big one. This might be the biggest benefit of learning a new language as it affects the learner the most profoundly. While the cognitive benefits of learning a language are too multifarious to all be mentioned within this book, some very important ones include: problem-solving and critical thinking skills, improved memory, ability to multitask, enhanced concentration, as well as better listening skills. Multilinguals also switch between monitor changes and competing tasks within their environments more easily than those who only speak one language. They also age more gracefully, with cognitive decline being staved off among the multilingual.

4. Exploring Other Cultures
To connect to a language is, in part, an effort to connect with the culture which surrounds the language. Learning another language can help teach the synthetic history and culture of a people, exposing the inquisitive student to every phase of activity such as tradition, religion, politics, philosophy, art, morals, and many more just through one medium.

5. Seeing the World through a Broader Lens
Multilingualism can make travelling around the world seem like an entirely different ballgame. Monolingual tourists tend to get trapped in tourist bubbles, only being allowed access to the aspects of the culture that foreigners get, while never getting the bigger picture that only the native language speakers can provide. Learning the language can open doors especially in terms of getting to know other people. Learning it can also provide more opportunities for studying and working abroad.

6. Seeing the Source
In the internet age, it is easy to confound fantasy with reality. When it comes to foreign nations, the internet (or any other source) can simply not compare to the real thing in terms of value, importance, or accuracy. Learning a language is a great key to the heart of the nation, and accuracy of one's understanding of it.

7. Becoming a Polyglot

Learning a second language is a useful feat, multiplying vocabulary and improving communication skills in one's native language. Learning languages beyond the second, however, has surprisingly been shown to be easier than it is the first time around. This is especially true for children; they are nature's greatest linguists. Once the neural networks involved in the process of new language acquisition have been primed, it is much easier for people to pick up more and more words from more and more obscure vernaculars.

8. A Major Boost of Confidence

At least as far as Americans are concerned, multilingualism is tantamount regality, and those who can display the skill have been shown to receive massive gains of social currency. While the inevitable mistakes which are made in the process of learning the language can tend to damage one's ego, these are offset by the self-worth gains that come with the territory. To learn a new language is an act of escaping one's comfort zone. After all, it is the satisfaction of learning a new language that can and will get the learner through the difficult precipitate phase of learning.

9. The Strengthening of Decision Making Abilities

Interestingly enough, it has been proven that decisions made in a person's second language are much more reason-based than those made in the native language. It is always funny how life always leaves us with more reason as time goes by. When deliberations are made in second and third tongues, emotional responses and biases connected with our mother tongue leave our thinking patterns more readily. It becomes much easier to be objective when speaking new languages because baggage dissolves and all that is left are facts and stratagem.

10. The Gaining of Perspective

As people embark on new journeys into novel cultures and places, familiarity always catches the senses. Common threads are observed by people that came out of their comfort zones and stayed there for a while. When this happens, it gives the much needed perspective on our native culture by making the learner reexamine things familiar to them in new lights. This is similar to measures taken by many dream therapists when dealing with patients with childhood baggage. The aspects of their dreams are asked to be described as if the patient were describing them to someone from another planet. By doing this, the patient can gain perspective on what inhabits their dreams and how they really feel about the things that they are exposed to in their waking lives. It gives opportunity to see the things around them in a new light and travelling abroad can do just that as well.

All the reasons for learning a foreign language listed above apply to any given language, but the next portion of this chapter will discuss the inner workings of the German language.

German

The Germanic language family is a very wide one which encompasses a wide variety of languages and dialects. The three major branches within this family are West Germanic languages, North Germanic languages, and East Germanic languages. Together, these branches are spoken by approximately 515 million people worldwide. Most of these people, however, reside in Europe.

The first branch to be mentioned here is the western branch of languages. This branch includes German, Dutch, English, Afrikaans (a descendant of Dutch), Low German, Yiddish, Scots, Limburgish varieties (with speakers along the borders of the Netherlands, Belgium, and Germany), and Frisian languages (with speakers in the Netherlands and Germany).

The northern branch is a much smaller one. Its languages include Icelandic, Norwegian, Swedish, Faroese, and Danish.

Lastly, we come to the Eastern branch of the language and are met by a graveyard of European tongues. The languages of this branch include Gothic, Vandalic, and Burgundian. All of these languages are now extinct, and the last one of them to die was the Crimean Gothic, which went in the late 18th century in rural parts of Crimea.

By most estimates, this family of languages consists of 48 individual living languages. Of these 48, 41 are listed as West Germanic languages, 6 are North Germanic languages, and 1 other language residing in Brazil which is the Riograndenser Hunsrükisch German, usually falls into neither category. It is now impossible to say just how many languages have been a part of this family throughout the course of history. Many of them, especially the East German languages, died out during or after the migration period following the decline of the Roman Empire between the fourth and sixth centuries A.D. Some West Germanic languages died out during this period as well, Lombardic would be one example.

World War 2 changed lots of things, including the German language. In linguistics, a *sprachraum* is defined as being a geographical region in which a common first language along with its dialect varieties is spoken. The *sprachraum* of the German family of languages suffered heavy losses in both area and speaker population as a result of World War 2. Meanwhile, the 21st century hasn't been much better for these dialects because many of them are dying out to make room for Standard German and its massive popularity in these regions.

The patriarch of this massive family is what was known as Proto-Germanic, or Common Germanic. This was a language spoken around the middle of the first millennium B.C. in what history remembers as Iron Age Scandinavia. This language, along with its numerous ancestors, is known for having a great number of linguistic features peculiar to it. One famous example among these is what is known as Grimm's Law. It is a consonant change completely unique to the Germanic family of languages. This Proto-Germanic language was later followed up by many varieties of the tongue, which travelled south of Scandinavia when several Germanic tribes in the 2nd century B.C. conquered and settled in many parts of modern northern Germany and southern Denmark.

A fourth century A.D. translation of the New Testament into Gothic is the earliest Germanic text known to history. This text was translated by Ulfilas, a Cappadocian Greek who worked as a missionary and bishop. Around the 10th century, the dialects varied so much that inter comprehensibility had become impossible, which is still true to this day. Again, the migration period culled off the East German languages, but they continued to influence the languages that surrounded them by assimilating themselves near their respective ends.

The middle ages then saw West German languages split between those which observed the new consonant shift, and those which didn't. The North German languages, on the other hand, stayed essentially united.

Any changes which occurred during and after (if such a time exists) the age of reason are relatively miniscule and more or less subordinate to those made beforehand. Most of these newer changes are due to standardization decrees and solutions to ongoing problems regarding certain aspects of the existing languages; Germanic languages are not born or culled off anymore, at least not for now.

Standard German

The first subset of the German language that it is necessary to go over here is so-called 'standard' German. This is a variety of the German language that has undergone standardization and is a common means of communication between some certain dialect areas. It is what was known as a Dachsprache or an Ausbau language serving as an independent variety of the language with other Abstand or dependent language varieties related to it. The role that Ausbau languages play for linguistics is that of builder-out or patriarch of other languages in the family.

Standard German did not start out as a dialect common across multiple regions. It took hundreds of years to evolve as a written language, with its writers constantly making changes to it for its widespread comprehension. At around 1800, the people of northern

Germany that are speakers of Low Saxon languages, started to learn the language as a foreign one. It later traveled southward and completely annihilated many of the languages of southern Germany, leaving only some small and scattered enclaves of Low German in its wake. Ever since, it has remained the standard language of Germany and her people, uniting a wide variety of tribes and dialects under one cultural blanket. As of today, though, these local dialects are usually only used in informal and private speech, commonly limited to home settings.

There are a few nations that this language inhabits, and the language differs slightly in every single one. These countries are: Austria, Switzerland, and Germany. In addition to these variances, there are different varieties of Standard German within the nation of Germany. These varieties of Standard German differ mostly from one another in vocabulary and pronunciation, although in some cases variance occurs in grammar and orthography. The different varieties of the language are not so clearly discerned in written language, but their variances shine through more vividly when spoken.

The variations of Standard German are, however, not to be confused with the various dialects of German, despite their similarities and influence to each other. The main thing that separates the two is the fact that the varieties of the Standard German language stem from the common tradition of the written German language. The local dialects, on the other hand, have roots that go back much further than Standard German, before the unification of the written German language and, in the case of low German, these dialects can belong to entirely different languages.

The Standard German language has undergone numerous standardization changes within its lifespan. This started way back in the 16th century, with the Luther Bible of 1534. These changes continued up until 2006, when the last one occurred over disputes about spelling and the splitting of German words. These will probably continue in the future, as language is an entity that undergoes constant evolution.

Low German

Low German is what is known as a West German Language and it is most commonly spoken in two regions: Northern Germany and the northeastern region of The Netherlands. Being most closely related to Frisian and English, this language is part of the Ingaevonic or North Sea Germanic group of West Germanic languages.

The dialects of Low German spoken in The Netherlands are referred to only as being Low Saxon, but, on the other hand, the dialects of northwestern Germany (Bremerhaven, Bremen, Hamburg, Westphalia, Schleswig-Holstein, and Lower Saxony) can be referred to as either being Low Saxon or Low German. Those spoken in northeastern Germany are exclusively Low German. These differences are a result of history; northwestern Germany as well as The Netherlands were once settlements of The Saxons, while northeastern Germany was not.

Old Saxon is the grandfather of Low German. It was spoken between the 9th and 12th centuries by the Saxon inhabitants of northwest Germany and Denmark. This language was survived by Middle Low German, spoken between 1100 and 1600. This language was neighbored by Middle Dutch in the west and by Middle High German in the south. Middle Low German is important historically because it served the Hanseatic league—a confederation of guilds and market towns throughout northwestern Europe in the late 1100s—as its *Lingua Franca* or *bridge language,* which supplied a common tongue throughout the confederation.

And to that end, we reach the contemporary situation of Low German. The Dutch and German dialects remain detached, and the decision to exclude the teaching of Low German throughout the schools of Germany was met with bitter opposition by some. Proponents of the teaching of the language argued on the point of its dense historical and cultural significance that it should remain in formal education. Meanwhile, High German had already become the widely used language in education, science, politics, and national unity. It was no wonder that High German would eventually win the day.

Low German has always played second fiddle to High German. Known for its archaic constructions and features, many linguists find this language backward and of limited use. Public reverence coupled with tradition have, however, kept the language afloat though. Today, while not being widely used in academia or in the professional world, Low German still finds itself in the homes of thousands of German speakers in spite of its supposed shortcomings. And, while it is still not widely taught, it also finds itself within the schools of Germany and The Netherlands.

High German

And finally, we at last come to Low German's more popular cousin, High German. High German refers to a variety of German dialects spoken in central as well as southern Germany, Austria, Switzerland, Liechtenstein, and Luxembourg. It also encompasses dialects spoken within regions of France (northern Lorraine and Alsace), The Czech Republic (Bohemia), Italy (south Tyrol), and Poland (upper Silesia). As with other European dialects, these ones are also spoken within various diaspora across the globe, namely in Romania, The United States, Brazil, Russia, Argentina, Chile, Mexico, and Namibia.

The main thing that differentiates High German from other forms of German dialects is the famous High German consonant shift.

The term 'High' German derives from the highlands of Germany, where these dialects originate from. This class of languages includes the famous Yiddish language of the Ashkenazi community of Jews in central Europe, standard German, and Luxembourgish. These aforementioned highlands of Germany are not limited to German soil however. They also include Luxembourg, Liechtenstein, Austria, and most of Switzerland. Meanwhile, its cousin Low German refers to dialects spoken in the lowlands of Germany and the Netherlands, along the coasts of the North German Plain.

This dialect can trace its roots back to around 500 A.D. in Old High German. In Old High German, two varieties, Swabian and East Franconian, became the dominant court and poetry languages of the House of Hohenstaufen around 1200. This term 'High German' introduces itself to history around 1400 in Upper Saxony, Swabia, Bavaria, Franconia, and Austria. This language triumphed over all those around it and continues to triumph today as an important basis of the German language.

It would now be wise to look over the family tree that all these dialects of German stem from. The other variants of the German language which have been mentioned previously are all related to this one, and is found within the large barge of central European languages. This tree of languages is roughly as follows:

Central German:
East Central German-
Upper Saxon
Thuringian
Lausitzisch-Neumärkisch
High Prussian
Silesian
West Central German-
Central Franconian
Moselle Franconian
Ripuarian
Rhine Franconian
Palatine
Hessian

High Franconian:
East Franconian
South Franconian

Upper German:
Alemannic-
Low Alemannic

High Alemannic
Highest Alemannic
Swabian
    Bavarian-
Central Bavarian
Northern Bavarian
Southern Bavarian
Hutterite German
Cimbrian

Yiddish
Lombardic (extinct)

Chapter 2:
Finding your passion for learning German

Studying outside of what is required in school can seem somewhat intimidating and time consuming. A great number of people seem to get the idea that informal and or unguided study can muddy up intellectual waters or otherwise just make it harder to learn. There are some grains of truth in this presumption, although in other cases, informal study can be more beneficial and efficient than its formal counterpart. It all depends on the student's erudition, work ethic, and grit more than anything. While it is typically advisable to study German (or any other subject for that matter) with some sort of teacher or tutor guiding you through the process, it remains more important that the student genuinely enjoys and takes an active interest in the field of study.

In this chapter we will take some time to discuss some studying tips and techniques that certainly prove to be useful when studying German, or any other subject for that matter.

The first, and a very important tip about studying that should be mentioned here is the practice of breaking the material, whatever it may be, into chunks that are more easily digestible. This is a practice that is especially useful for working on a task that seems overwhelming. Once the material has been carved out into smaller sections, those individual sections can be studied with more ease from day to day. This can take superfluous pressure off of the student and allow for better focus on the tasks at hand.

Another important tip would be to reward yourself for hard work done. It doesn't, after all, make someone self-indulgent or weak to reap the rewards of his or her labor. These small rewards can actually be beneficial and can be done in the forms of short walks, small blocks of phone time, or maybe even the occasional snack in between longer periods of study.

Human beings are creatures of habit, which is exactly why it can be extremely useful to create a routine of creating your own study time (or work hours for that matter). These habits, in fact, can become so strong that it can even become difficult for a student to be able to relax for the day without studying first. With constant and prolonged self-discipline, any given person can become a student to be reckoned with, leaving all competition in the dust. Studies show, however, that it takes 20 to 30 days on average to form a habit, which is why self-discipline should be duly emphasized.

For those still in school, it is important to be clear with yourself when it comes to why you want to get good grades. It is always easier to meet your goals when there is a general idea of why those goals should be met. One useful method of doing this is making a list of academic and personal goals, for example:

I would like to develop myself and learn more.
I would like to get into more useful habits.
I would like to become more disciplined and focused as a student.
I would like to get into a good school.
I would like to have a good career one day.
I would like to provide for my family and those who are close to me in the future.
I would like to have certainty that I'm doing all that I can in my endeavors.
I would like to live as regret free as I possibly can.

Writing goals and aspirations down can give perspective and direction for the student. Also, the lists made can serve as reminders and motivators in the future.

The use of mind maps is a very good skill for students to have. Unlike lists, mind maps allow interconnectivity that the brain always craves. These can be used for any subject and under any circumstances and the outcomes always remain fruitful. The brain makes connections naturally, and mind maps not only assist in this process, but also defines and clarifies the connections made.

Another tip would be to try to always make a boring subject seem and feel as interesting as possible. This one can be particularly useful in learning German as many often consider learning foreign languages boring. It is always important, however, to stave off boredom when studying like the disease that it is. There are many methods of doing this successfully, but the most important one would be to re-engage yourself. No subjects are ultimately very boring at all as long as people just look over them with disinterested minds. It is always important to simply dig a little deeper every time the student feels like yawning.

It is always more advantageous, and also more rewarding, to come to understand topics rather than just memorizing their contents. Rote memorization can take a learner quite far, and there are always some bastions of employing this in your study habits, but in more advanced studies and inquisitive minds, it becomes increasingly important to grasp the material at hand as reference to other subjects. This is also more important than memorization because it actually makes room for critical thinking and the application of facts. In learning German, there is always emphasis placed on vocabulary, but there is also emphasis placed on actually putting the words together to make statements that makes sense.

Another important practice in learning is to always be on the lookout for personal knowledge gaps as well as thinking errors. There is, after all, no room for competence, or in this case fluency, where there remains an overabundance of mistakes. Staying cognizant of errors in learning will not only curtail mistakes and misunderstandings, but it will also deepen the student's understanding of the subject matter at hand.

Studying in shorter increments of time is always beneficial as well. This study habit has been shown to be more effective than others. It is what is known as *spaced* learning, and its advantages are attributed to the way memories are formed. Neurons have to be left alone for periods of time in between study for memories to be properly embedded within the links between them. This is why it is always beneficial to avoid cramming, so spaced learning would naturally be the best method of studying for the mind.

The Pomodoro Technique is a very famous yet not very widely used technique in learning. Its most basic and most common structure are as follows:

1. Decide on the task that you need to work.
2. Time yourself within a 25-minute increment .
3. Start working on the task.
4. Stop working once the 25-minute mark has been reached.
5. Checkmark a piece of paper.
6. If you are up to fewer than four check marks, then you must take a 3 to 5-minutes break, repeat from step one when your break has been completed.
7. After four check marks, or Pomodoros, have been met, you must then take a 15 to 30-minute break.
8. Draw a line crossing off the four check marks and start over again

This technique keeps the study blocks short and on point so that knowledge is retained well and the student is not fatigued.

Another important piece of advice is the fact that motivation should be expected to come frequently or readily. As strange as it may seem, motivation can generally come more readily when it is not expected or desired so much. It appears well by contrast, as with any other mood. No one among us feels motivated all the time, so it is not advisable to rely on feelings of motivation to retain the ability on getting things done. This is why it is more important to keep a strict routine and work through the boredom that surrounds studying.

It is important, maybe beyond any other tips listed here, to exercise the brain. In doing this, it can be helpful to look at the brain as a

muscle than an organ because it gives more of an impression of adaptability. Developing one's ability to focus is like any other form of personal development where in it takes constant practice and unflappable determination. It's like becoming a great athlete, it takes thousands of hours of practice that is set on a rigid schedule over the course of years. The only real difference is that it is the mind being worked out rather than the body. Some great means of developing this skill are challenging world issues, writing journals, or solving puzzles. The greater and wider the variety of ways that your brain is challenged, the stronger and more powerful it will become.
Here are some websites with great resources for training the brain: Luminosity, NeuroNation, and Brain HQ.

The roles of rest and recovery are also not to be underestimated in study. It is always important to get at least 8 hours of sleep each and every night, no matter what you spend your waking hours doing. There are also certain foods which are better for the health of the brain than others. Some foods that offer fatty acids which the brain needs to function properly are as follows:

Nuts, avocados, salmon, berries, beans, pumpkin seeds, pomegranate juice, and dark chocolate.

This next piece of advice ties in with the concept on creating a study routine very well. This one would be to organize your time. With creating a study schedule comes lots of commitment, and where commitment goes, motivation usually follows. It is always much easier to stay with a topic to keep an organized schedule. Here are some steps in creating a reliable study schedule:

1. Make a list of tasks which you need to complete for every subject that you study.
2. Try downloading a study schedule template or making one by hand. You can then block of available times for independent study.
3. Try to keep things simple and easy to remember by choosing blocks of time that remain the same throughout each day of the week.

4. Create a plan for every day which includes the most important tasks that the day has to offer, then make sure to stick to it religiously.

At the end of each week, or any allotted time frame, you can then track the progress that you have made. You may then be pleasantly surprised by your results, and if you are not, then you can always keep trying to make adjustments to whatever you need to to meet your goals.

The results of all these methods mentioned will ultimately all be dependent upon how hard the student tries. With that being said, it is always important to remain active in your learning experiences rather than passive. Passive learning takes on the presumption that the learner is a blank slate, but many attests that the best way to learn is to immerse oneself in learning completely. Here are some steps in doing this more effectively:

Finding applications of topics within your normal life
Performing case studies to test ideas and concepts Group projects
Brainstorming on ways to apply the concepts learned to the issues that you come across

All of these tips can be applied not only in your pursuit of learning German, but to virtually any subject the student takes up. German is one of the most important and useful languages of modernity, and in addition, it is a relatively easy language to learn for the native English speaker. By using these techniques in learning German or any other subject, the student will not only learn the subject with more ease, but also use the tools gained here to help him or her to develop other skills in the future. These are concepts that are stuck out of time and place. It is always much more useful to know how to learn than what to learn. Education is a constantly evolving chapter within a student's life, and one that can never quite be mastered, but can be rode to greater heights with proper practice and skill.

Chapter 3: Immersing yourself in German culture

German Culture
Germany is very much the center of Europe in more ways than just geographically. It also serves as the center of European economic and political activity. Germany is Europe's second most populous country in terms of overall population, behind Russia. In fact, the World Factbook estimates its population to be around 80 million people. Germany's economy also boasts impressive figures as well. It is, in fact, the largest one within the continent and the fifth largest one on the face of the globe.

Germany not only is home to an extremely large population, but it also exerts influence over many smaller nations that border it. These include Belgium, Czech Republic, Austria, Denmark, Luxembourg, France, Switzerland, The Netherlands, and Poland. All of these cultures listed have had reciprocal influence on and from Germany.

Unsurprisingly, the population of Germany is around 91.5%. It may, however, come as a bit of a shock to learn that the second largest ethnic group is actually Turkish at about 2.4% of the nation's population. This leaves a remaining 6.1% accounted to the different groups of ethnic Greek, Italian, Russian, Serbo-Croatian, and Spanish people. It is the city life which most of Germany's people are drawn to. However, roughly 75.7% of the population residing in urban areas.

The Germans are a very staid and conservative people, placing high values on the virtues of structure, punctuality, and privacy. Some of the stereotypes surrounding Germany and her people hold true in these few respects. They also place very high quotas on hard work, industriousness, and thriftiness. It takes a lot to make Germans comfortable, usually. They often need to have the ability to organize and compartmentalize the world into well-kept units, as they are a very pragmatic people. They therefore tend to manage their time rather carefully, with calendars, schedules, and agendas taking precedence over any spontaneity that life's vicissitudes have to offer.

The Germans often get the reputation of being rather stoic people. This is understandable as they do tend to strive for precision and perfection in nearly every aspect of their day to day lives. This is not always such a bad trait to have though. In fact, it's often a great one that has lots of practical benefits. Civilizations often begin as stoic and end up being epicurean. It could be argued that the only thing more destructive than access stoicism is mindless pleasure seeking. They seldom hand out compliments to others and even less seldom admit faults, even jokingly. These are aspects of their stoicism that could be criticized. All of these factors may coalesce to make these people seem unfriendly, but the Germans actually have very highly developed social consciences and keen senses of community.

Language
The main language of Germany, which is unsurprisingly German, has many different offshoots previously mentioned. Standard German is spoken by a landslide 95% of the population. Several minor languages including Low German, High German, Dutch, Frisian variances, and many more are also spoken in Germany.

Religion
Like the vast majority of the western world, Christianity dominates the land for centuries. This religion is followed by 65 to 70% of the nation. With that figure, Catholics comprise 29% of them. Meanwhile, Muslims are a small minority, as in lots of other European nations, accounting for 4.4% of the total population. The remaining 36% of the population are not religious or does not observe a religion other than those two previously mentioned.

The two largest churches in Germany are the Roman Catholic Church, and the Evangelical Church. Their Evangelical Church is a confederation of Protestant (Lutheran and Reformed) churches. Those two churches comprise the 65 to 70% of the nation. In 2016, Orthodox Christianity made up for around 2% of the overall population.

The religious makeup of the nation of Germany differs greatly with a number of factors, namely region and age. As could probably be expected, the youth are now less religious than their elders. In fact, the majority of Germany's population under 25 now claim to hold no religious belief. Another trend that is common in Germany, and also in many parts of the world, is the inverse correlation between urban living and religiosity. In fact, in many major German cities, Berlin and Hamburg for example, non-religious people comprise the majority of citizenry. As far as states are concerned, however, it is the Eastern states which hold the least religious belief. A majority of 60-70% classify as holding no religious belief in these states. Some of these figures seem surprising in contrast to American religiosity, but the culture of Germany doesn't seem to suffer much from the variance.

As is the case for most of the globe, Germany started out with polytheistic paganism and eventually adopted Christianity later. This occurred only in prehistoric Germany and parts of Scandinavia. The concept of a united German land just did not exist until Julius Caesar, invading Gaul, sought to destroy the increasingly united Germanic tribes above him. This primitive religion included Gods such as Thor, Odin, Freyja, and Baldr.

After the 4th century, in the regions of southern Germany which had then been occupied as part of the Roman Empire, early Christianity began to take hold and replaced the old Gods. Never again would these Gods rule German soil. Pagan temples and ways of life were then replaced by Christian churches and morality to uphold the sudden transition.

It was until the Carolingian Period, however, that Christianity began to take its hold over the German mainland. The main person responsible for this invasion was Charlemagne, with his swift military invasions followed by his conversion tactics. One great example of religious structures built during this time period is the Palace of Aachen, built during Charlemagne's reign.

The Germany of the middle ages then saw very little to virtually no change in its religious institutions. The majority of the region remained Roman Catholic and, for the most part, busied itself with issues other than official religion.

In 1517, Martin Luther published his 95 Theses, one of the most Seminole documents ever written throughout the history of the world. Its main objective was the criticism of the Roman Catholic Church for its selling of indulgences (payments made to clergy to atone for sins) along with other abuses of power.

Not only was Luther opposing how the clergy abused their powers at that time, but he was also opposing the very idea of the papacy. The Reformation is significant in that it is the first open criticism or reaction to the corruption and misguidance of the Roman Catholic Church known to history. The publication of the theses was quickly followed up by the Diet of Worms in 1521, which outlawed Luther. The Reformation continued regardless and would not rest until it had consumed all of Europe open to its teachings. Luther followed up by then translating the bible from Latin to German, making it readable and accessible to all people of all German speaking regions of Europe, not just the clergy. This in turn made the bible much more approachable to Europe and gave the Roman Catholic Church much less power of its teachings. Today, the denominations of Christianity are so numerous that no one has very much theological power over the religion. How Luther turns out to be important in linguistic history is the fact that the dialect that he translated the bible into was not by any means a widespread or popular one before his translation, now it has evolved into Standard German.

After the Thirty Years War, there was a widespread effort to unite the larger Lutheran and the smaller Reformed Protestant Churches. This occurred in Prussia, with King Frederick William III's motivation being the unification of all protestant churches within the nation under the crown. This was done with several complications, and eventually Frederick William IV had to give the 'Old' Lutherans the right to separate from this conglomeration in an effort to keep peace among the public.

This point in religious history marks a widespread attitude shift in relation to God. The Roman Catholic Church placed more emphasis on worship, ceremony, and the church, but followers of the new denominations were searching for more personal relationships with God. The German people, whether out of hubris or out of need for personal growth, started to see God as wanting a personal relationship with his children. This is a view that many of these denominations still hold today.

As the rationalism of the 18th century eventually faded away, the individualism of the 19th century continued to shape Germany's concept of God. All of this was, of course, met by fierce opposition from Catholics still loyal to the papacy. There was then a controversy surrounding children of mixed marriages. There was no consensus on what the legal religion of children born to both Catholic and Protestant parents should be. After some deliberation, it was decided that these children should always be raised Protestant. This differed from the Napoleonic laws previously set in place which ordered that the parents should be the one making the decision on what will be the religion of mixed children.

The most crucial blow to the power of the papacy, however, came in the human form of Otto von Bismarck, who flatly refused to tolerate any given power base outside of Germany to have a say in German affairs. Bismarck launched a so called 'culture war' against the power of the pope in 1873, which gained lots of support among German liberals opposing the power of the church.

From that point on, although they comprised about a third of the German population, Catholics were not allowed to hold most offices within the German and Prussian governments. This is, however, overshadowed by the fact that after 1871 a systematic purge of Catholics began within the two nations. In fact, the interior ministry at the time only staffed one Catholic boy in total. Another religious minority discriminated against the Jews throughout this time.

One of the ways in which this purge of Catholics was achieved was through what is now known as the Pulpit Law. This law prohibited the use of speech by clergy which in any way displeased the government. Many officials within the Roman Catholic Church were openly against this law, and many of them were imprisoned or exiled as a result.

Bismarck did, however, severely underestimated the power and tenacity of the Catholic people in their resistance to his exclusive laws. The Catholic Church promptly denounced these new laws and called upon its followers in all parts of Germany to protest the treatment. An uneasy peace was eventually established as some of these laws were repealed, but several discriminatory laws regarding education and work were left in place.

The newly formed Weimar Republic established a constitution for itself in 1919 which not only did not include any official state religion, but also guaranteed freedom of faith and religion to all its citizens. Earlier in German history, these freedoms had only been mentioned in the constitutions of some individual states. Catholics and Protestants were finally equal under the letter of the law with this new constitution. The German Freethinkers League was then established. It was comprised of 500,000 members, mostly atheist. Nazi leadership did, fittingly enough, shut this group down later in 1933.

The year 1933 marked one of the most important and devastating times in the history of Germany. In January of that year, Adolf Hitler's Nazi Party seized control of the German government seeking to assert state control over the churches among other things. Two social responses to this were the Positive Christianity and Deutsche

Christen movements, which both sought to the tenants of National Socialism with the Christian religion. These movements had mixed successes until the late 1936, when gradual worsening of relations between the church and state caused many to abandon the churches. There were no official policies regarding church membership within the Nazi government, but many officials started to leave their churches in droves around this time. Jews at this time were, as the reader already knows, increasingly marginalized as well.

The conclusion of World War 2 saw the German state divided into two parts: East and West. West Germany was now controlled by the western allies, namely England, America, France, and Canada. Eastern Germany, on the other hand, was now controlled by the U.S.S.R. East and West Germany now took two completely different approaches on the issue of religious freedom. West Germany, otherwise known as the Federal Republic of Germany, adopted a constitution in 1949 which stated that no citizen was to be discriminated against on the basis of their faith or religious beliefs, and that no official state religion was to be established. East Germany, also known as the German Democratic Republic, adopted a communist system which aimed to drastically reduce the role of religion in the society. Christian churches, regardless of denomination, were restricted by the government. This explains the aforementioned tendency of eastern German states to be less religious. The implications of soviet policies are still seen today.

German religious communities of a sufficient size and stability that happen to be loyal to the constitution are what is known as statutory corporations. These communities are given special privileges under the constitution. Included within these is the right for state schools to give religious instruction within these communities. They are also subject to having membership fees collected (for various fees) by the national revenue department known as 'church taxes'. These taxes are surcharges between 8 and 9% of the income tax. This differs from many other western nations which don't typically tax their churches. This high status applies mainly to the Roman Catholic Church, the mainline Protestant Evangelical Church in Germany, various free churches throughout the nation, and a small number of Jewish communities. There is also the ongoing discussion over whether or not to allow Muslims and other minority religious groups into this system as well.

In 2018, representatives from Schleswig-Holstein, Hamburg, Lower Saxony, and Bremen have come together to conclude that a decision on whether or not to make Reformation Day an official holiday permanently was desperately needed to be ratified by their state parliaments. This initiative began after the 500th anniversary of the reformation in 2017. It also stems, in part, from the fact that the northern German states now have far less holidays annually than many of the southern states do. Also during this year, the states of Schleswig-Holstein, Hamburg, Lower Saxony, and Bremen all adopted resolutions and made it an official holiday.

In contemporary times, Protestantism dominates the north and east of Germany and Catholicism dominates the south and west. The decline of Christianity in the late 20th and early 21st centuries, coupled with the state atheism of the former German Democratic Republic, have merged to create an extremely secular culture in northeastern Germany. The late 20th and the early 21st centuries have, however, brought immigrants from a wide variety of foreign lands and they brought with them lots of religions and beliefs that are new to the nation. These include Eastern Orthodox Christianity and Islam.

Cuisine
German cuisine may often be overshadowed by its neighbors such as France, Italy, and even England, but that does not imply that German cuisine is by any means worse. German cuisine is probably most widely known for its hardiness and its boldness. It's also more meat-oriented as compared to many of its European cousins. Of all meats, pork is the most widely consumed in Germany. Braised pork hock (schweinshaxe) and pork stomach (saumagen) are two of Germany's favorite dishes.

On the subject of sausage, the bratwurst may be the most famous food Germany has to offer. The nation is also rather fond of cabbage, turnips, and beets in its meals. Potatoes and sauerkraut are also immensely popular staples of the German cuisine, as well as cuisines of the world over.

The most popular alcoholic beverage in Germany is undoubtedly beer, and the nation serves as a home to lots of different varieties of the drink. Yes! The Germans love their beer about as much as life itself in some cases. Some of the varieties of beer that Germany has produced are Pilsner, Weizenbier, and Alt, all of which were originally made in ordinance with 'purity law' of 16th century Bavaria that mandated brews to be made only with hops, barley, and water. Schnapps and Brandy are also very popular in Germany.

Art
When one thinks of artistic contributions made on German soil, composers are usually the first people who come to mind. Beethoven, Bach, and Mozart (even though he was Austrian) immediately pop into anyone's head. And perhaps the classical music buff even recalls the works of Schoenberg, Alban Berg, and the other late composers of The Second Viennese School. When all of these giants are considered, it becomes more obvious that many believe that it was Germany who dominated most stages of classical music, but Germany's artistic output is not limited just to music.

Workforce
Germany, with its stolid value placed on precision and detail, has gained quite a reputation as a great home to highly skilled engravers and woodcutters. In addition to their contributions to these art forms, they are also known for architectural works of great importance. Their output in architecture has been strong for centuries now, surviving and even thriving throughout the Romanesque, Gothic, Classicist, Baroque, Rococo, and Renaissance periods. These works have taken numerous forms, including cathedrals, public buildings, and even castles. The Brandenburg Gate

comes to mind as one of the many examples of the classical German style.

The German desire for orderliness and exactitude invades each and every facet of the life of the nation. This phenomenon is not by any means divorceable from the working life of Germany either, including the business sector. It is widely known among Germans that surprise, humor, or anything even remotely tongue and cheek is not typically welcomed among the businessmen and women of Germany. They are the most pragmatic and conscientious people. Every moment of the waking life of the business class workers are carefully planned and decided upon beforehand. Every moment leads up to the next, with little to no room for variance when it comes to decisions which have already been made.

Engineers are highly esteemed in German culture, and also very well paid at that. This comes as no surprise when considering some of the traits that engineers all have in common: analytical and management skills, attention to detail, and conscientiousness. This is also evidenced clearly by Germany's continuing success in the automotive industry. This nation has lots of respect for hands on expertise, a quality that is usually not very appreciated in the west anymore. This is why professionals with this trait typically do better in the business world of Germany than those who can only boast a financial or educational background.

The German workforce also values diligence and competence over interpersonal skills. This is one trait which Germany shares with most of its western neighbors. The German people are not highly regarded as being very diplomatic or friendly in their speech with coworkers, clients, or other outsiders. They are, above all, direct in these instances.

All traits and factors may culminate to give the impression that the German workforce is a dismal, even dreary entity. There may be some grains of truth in this, as work in Germany is no picnic, but it would not be fair to assert that Germany is much worse than her neighbors when it comes to her workers' wellbeing.

Germany is, in fact, one of the best places to work in here in the western world. A person just needs to become accustomed to the business culture of the nation. Germans may at first seem to foreigners sensible, punctual, reserved, precise, target-oriented, cold, arrogant, obedient, sure of themselves, disciplined, plan-oriented, stiff, unfeeling, authoritative, bureaucratic, direct, professional, self-assured, correct, petty, strong, highly orderly, humorless, reliable, principled, perfectionist, and organized.

These stereotypes may reflect the reality of the culture. They also are rooted in cultural standards which perform their functions on a generalized and abstract level. While they may be bothersome and frustrating at times, they ultimately serve better functions than what meets the eye.

Some of the most important cultural standards which Germany adheres to are as follows:

The task at hand is the religion of the people. It takes precedence over all other things and determines the language and dispositions of all workers. The task at hand should, therefore, be focused on more so than anything else. This includes relationships. Relationships in the business world of Germany take on a subordinate role to work, as they probably should.

German business is widely known for its arguably excessive processes, procedures, rules, and regulations. The businessmen and women of Germany value the application of and adherence to contracts and written agreements very highly. Rigid consequences and sometimes harsh penalties are what those who diverge from the contents of these understandings are met with. This fact highlights at once the importance of mutual obligation and the lack of flexibility and individual determination within the business world of Germany.

Consistency and reliability are minor deities to the German business class. Rule orientation and internalized focus of control also serve important functions within the happenings of the German business world. With so much emphasis placed on the importance of structure and order, it comes as no surprise to us to learn that Germans are never open to welcome uncertainty. They therefore prefer binding rules and agreements to curtail any chances of being caught off guard.

German punctuality is also impressive in its widespread application and quotidian adherence. Meetings and appointments are strictly planned, and their times are met with promptitude and certainty. They follow their schedules tightly to ensure certainty in dealing with one another.

With all these constrictions and rigid regulations, it becomes of the utmost importance to separate the private sphere of regular life with the public sphere of business life. The culture just doesn't allow for as much personality to merge between the two. It would make personal life too austere and professional life too free. With this being said, there is made very little room for friendship within the business world of Germany. This is one of the reasons why German workers often get the reputation of being unfriendly and aloof among their foreign coworkers.

And finally, the last point that should be made on the subject of German business is that of the directness of communication within the German business world. Germanic speech is known for being very direct to the point, without any 'dressing' or sugar coating of any sort. This has lots of practical advantages, making language much more explicit and useful, but it can also give off the impression of coldness and unfriendliness. This is just another example of the unique cultural standards of Germany though. And, as with others, it has its merits and demerits alike.

Holidays and Celebrations
Germany, being a predominantly Christian nation, celebrates many of the same holidays that other Christian nations in the west usually

do, including Christmas, Easter, and Good Friday. There are also a few holidays and celebrations unique to German culture, including German Unification Day on October 3rd, a recent holiday celebrating the unification of post war East and West Germany.

The longest, and perhaps most famous, of all German celebrations is Oktoberfest. This festival starts on a specific Saturday in September and ends 16 to 18 days later on the first Sunday of October. This is a celebration marked with and known for lots of drunken revelry and jollity. It started in the year 1810 with a massive celebration of the marriage between Ludwig of Bavaria and Therese Von Sachsen Hildburghausen.

Chapter 4:
Finding native speakers to increase your overall understanding of the language and culture

Much like learning a first language, learning a second one takes lots of practice and time. It is rather hard to imagine learning a first language while remaining taciturn around speakers of that language, so why would a student restrain his or her self to silence in the process of learning any language beyond that? It hits all the bull's eye on all the wrong targets to learn a second language without using it for communication, after all, what else is language good for? Learning and speaking a second language also provides opportunity to learn about other cultures from people with potential first-hand experience with the given culture, German in this case. The benefits of practicing a foreign language far outweigh the costs under virtually any given circumstances.

Speaking a foreign language with others can streamline so much of the learning process. It can undermine so much of the complexity and nuance involved in language acquisition, and in a way that won't jeopardize educational value or accuracy, depending on the person being spoken to. Even speaking with one person who knows German or any other foreign language can expose the student to the entirety of that person's vernacular. The speech can be absorbed and digested naturally. The zone of proximal development, a zone discovered by Piaget in which children are naturally given just a little bit more information that they can fully understand, also applies to people learning a second language. It is really just like any other skill in the sense that it really takes practice and patience to develop.

One important reason why communicating using the second language with others works is the complexity of grammatical forms in virtually any language. This makes it difficult or even impossible to fully learn a language. In fact, linguists have not yet been able to fully describe all the grammatical constructs of even a single language. While speaking with another person may not completely run off grammatical difficulties, it can curtail some of the more embarrassing mistakes that can be made. It could also be added that learning from a native speaker can imbue the student with some of the education that the speaker has received, in a way giving the student a formal education by proxy.

While constant studying effort and rote memorization are important factors in learning a new language, the two take on subordinate roles to what is said to the student and what the student reads. These two are the most important factors in new language acquisition. They work together to supply a more useful comprehensible input than other methods of learning do. As the student receives more and more comprehensible input through reading and listening to the language, it becomes easier and easier to absorb more of the vocabulary and grammar of the second language. It creates a self-sustaining positive feedback loop that can end in fluency easier than the average learner expects.

When learning a new language, it is important not to fluster oneself. Studies have on occasion shown that memorizing vocabulary and intensive grammar study are of limited value when compared to other methods of learning. Again, the importance of comprehensive input becomes so clear here. Students in classes more oriented towards comprehensive input than traditional grammar-based classes do better on communication, and even grammar-based tests across the board. These students get the benefits of a learning experience closer to natural education and can easily apply their skills on their own and in the world. In addition, they are even more likely to continue to study foreign languages.

Comprehensive input also plays a major role (if not, the main role) in vocabulary expansion of any language learned. Many multilinguals build up, as the reader can already guess, enormous vocabularies in each and every language that they learn. These huge collections of verbiage have a tendency to accumulate and expand on top of themselves with the passage of time. But this is seldom done with rote vocabulary memorization. These collections of words are almost always the result of comprehensive input over time. Reading is, of course, always important here as well. One study actually showed that people who spoke Spanish as a second language and also happened to read avidly in fact accumulated larger Spanish vocabularies than native Spanish speakers who did not read often.

Whenever a student learns a second language, it is only natural that he or she will tend to be taciturn at times during the beginning stages. These 'quiet periods' are a useful and protective tool in learning, and are typically more common in children, though adults experiencing these should not feel discouraged for doing so. Also, there are no comprehensive input teaching methods which require their students to speak the languages. It is ultimately not very relevant whether or not the student speaks the language openly, although pronunciation could be a hurdle in speaking with others.

The forcing of students to speak when they are not comfortable doing so not only makes them uncomfortable, but it also does virtually nothing for new language acquisition. The ability to speak the language in itself is a result of comprehensive input. A student can avoid learning a new language through trial and error by speaking it as he or she had to do with the first language that he or she had learned. This will bring no setbacks and can even help the student in the learning process.

Speaking with people in German can seem intimidating, out of social apprehension or fear of embarrassment, but there are many ways to get around these barriers that are destructive in language learning. One way, maybe the easiest or the most useful, to circumnavigate these problems is to text people in German. This is one practice which can be especially helpful for those who don't live in German speaking nations and who may not live around very many others who speak German. It cuts distances to nothing and makes communication all the more approachable and accessible.

HelloTalk is a new app and website which provides a great service for those wishing to connect with people across different languages. Meeting new German speaking buddies is fast and easy as this website is designed for learners aiming to set up new language exchanges.

Meeting native German speakers on this website is very simple. Most, if not all, the users of this website are incredibly enthusiastic and dedicated, so it is to be expected that a student will find people who will help and motivate him or her and expand horizons for the both of them. It is much like many forms of social media, the user can search for other language learners' information to find (in this case) native German speakers, or the user can submit his or her own information and wait to be found by another language learner.

German is just one of over 100 different language options on this website, so any user wishing to find speakers of any other language will have plenty of options. It is all completely free to send messages, make phone calls, or engage in any other forms of communication through this website, so connecting with the German speaking world is almost as easy here as it is in German speaking Europe.

If the idea of phone calls or verbal communication in German fills you with reticence, then HelloTalk is a great app for you to download. This app will read whatever text you submit to it aloud in German with the correct pronunciation used. This is especially useful in getting an idea of the flow of the language and, of course, the pronunciation of its words.

Another great feature that this app has to offer is a feature in which you can say whatever words or phrases into the microphone of your computer and it will type whatever is said back to you in German or another language of your choice. This app will even go so far as to correct your spelling and grammar along the way. If you are ever at a loss as far as translations to or from German are concerned, this app can be a very useful resource to you.

Another useful (and somewhat fun) method to use when learning German with native speakers is the practice of alternating between German and English. If slots of time are divided up between the two languages, let us say 10-20 minutes for example, greater results can typically be produced. The speakers won't be as fatigued by longer slots of time and they will have an easier time focusing on the languages spoken. As was mentioned before, it is always beneficial to study in shorter periods of time to consolidate memories more effectively. On the other hand, it is also beneficial to increase the amount of time spoken incrementally each day or so to build endurance and skill in speaking the language.

While this strategy may be only for the outgoing and the less timid among us, it is still a very useful one at that. Speaking to strangers can be one of the more exciting and novel means of learning a new language. Conversely though, this can also be a great method for those who are shy as well. The greatest thing about speaking with strangers is that strangers have no idea who you are and most of them will never see you twice. This is great for people with social anxiety surrounding speaking a foreign language because it takes so much pressure off the speaker. As an added bonus, this is a great way to potentially make new friends as people are often very charmed by seeing a non-native speaker trying to tackle such a complex and nuanced language.

One aspect of learning a new language is the inevitable accent disparity that is bound to come up in speaking. This is not something which should be a concern by the student though. It is nearly impossible to master an accent typical of a foreign tongue. Most can't even master their own regional accent and have practically no reason for doing so. While it is natural to be self-conscious of how one sounds to others, especially when speaking a second or third language, it is not always rational to place too much emphasis on this. Most people will either not notice a foreign accent, or not pay much attention to it. What is always more important is that the content is understandable and relatively clear. Other than that, it becomes important not to terrorize oneself into silence.

Circumlocution is a great skill to use in learning a new language. This is also a skill that would be beneficial to use in one's native language as well. It is not always practical to search for direct translations of every single word when learning the vocabulary of a new language. It can be somewhat tedious. If words are navigated towards the use of context and comparison then not only can communication be made easier, but new pathways can be formed by the use of the connections made. It is like thinking in of itself, it is better to know *how* to think than to know *what* to think. Navigating through content towards the appropriate words in a given situation can help the learner to develop skills in language learning in the future.

The hardest part of speaking to someone in a second or third language is always the beginning. This is the case in learning any language period. But it is important to remember that this small apprenticeship does not last forever, and that once something close to fluency is established, it will be retained in the mind with less effort than it took to absorb. The most important thing here is, as always, persistence. While learning with another may initially be intimidating and difficult, it is the offer of a delayed reward which should keep the learner in the game. It is not hard at all to give up here and sometimes extremely hard to stick to studying, so persistence, again, remains of paramount importance.

Chapter 5:
How to beat the most difficult part of learning the German language

The beginning stages

It is possible and feasible to learn the German language quickly. The most difficult parts, however, are the beginning stages. Once these stages have been completed, the learning curve increases dramatically, but first it is necessary to cross the first few humps in learning German. These can be beset on every side by pitfalls and mistakes just waiting to be made by the new language learner, which is why it is important to remain cognizant of all facets of the language at hand, and to consider practicing with others for additional editing and advice.

Regardless of your reasons for learning German, whether you have German-speaking friends or relatives, or have been drawn in by the famously strange and intimidatingly long words of the language, it still remains possible to learn the language at your own pace and on your own time.

The freedom to learn this language on your own time, however, comes with responsibility. It still remains important to study persistently in these initial stages, erring on the side of brevity, but also remaining thorough in your study of the language. The utility of speaking the language with friends, acquaintances, and strangers, as well as one website have all been mentioned before. There are, however, other means of learning the language which are equally practical and accessible in which should be mentioned here:

Audio courses, CD programs, and online radio
Internet-based games, and grammar books
Tablet and smartphone apps

German language movies and TV shows
German language books, magazines, and newspapers
Immersion and getting involved with the culture

Again, HelloTalk and other apps and websites like it are also great resources in learning the language. Here you can connect with native German speakers, as well as other language learners, 24/7 for free. This may prove to be more beneficial than any of the resources mentioned above due to the opportunity to connect with others through the language.

One aspect of the German language that is very beneficial to the native English speaker wishing to learn German is that the German language is very closely related to English. This can prove to be very much a head start in the acquisition of the new language. This is also especially important in the initial stages of learning the German language. If vocabulary and grammar of the German language are studied for virtually any period of time, any given English speaker will be able to draw parallels between the two languages with ease. This makes connection forming and inference patterns much easier for the learner to develop. Some native speaker of a language from a different family—a native Japanese speaker for instance—would have a much more difficult time learning German or any other Germanic language than a native English speaker would.

One of the most difficult things for any speaker learning German, however, is Germanic grammar. The main thing that differentiates Germanic grammar from the grammar of lots of other languages is the fact that it seldom changes a large chunk. If not all, most of the grammatical structure which belongs to the German language dates back to the fully inflected modes of the language's ancestry. This grammar is very similar to that of Latin, Greek, and old Russian.

One aspect of this grammar that is incredibly dissimilar to English grammar is sentence structure. Sentences in German are structured in completely different ways than they are in English. This makes parallel or word by word translations of full sentences either ill-advised, or simply impossible, which is just one of the innumerable reasons why the power of inference is so important in learning German or any other language, for that matter. One example of these differences could be: 'someone help me' would turn into 'Jemand hilf mir', which would literally turn into 'someone me help' in English.

As you can see, the grammatical side of the German language is probably the most difficult aspect of the language from a native English speakers' point of view. However, as with all other facets of learning this language, once the ropes have been shown to the learner it becomes much easier to navigate through speaking the language.

It would now prove useful to include a few important first steps in learning this language. These are as follows:

Master the alphabet

The best first step that a student can make in learning a foreign language is pouring over the language's alphabet and finding the similarities and dissimilarities between that language and the student's native language. It is the letters with umlauts (two dots over them) which should have special attention drawn to them. These change the pronunciation of the letters, and therefore how the entirety of the word sounds. Another quirk in German pronunciation, as in English pronunciation, is the drawing together of two letters to produce sounds much different from the sums of their parts. These are also things to watch out for in the initial stages of learning German.

Learn easy words first

Once the alphabet is mastered, it finally becomes possible to move on to the more entertaining period of learning actual words. These first and easiest words are what are known as 'framework' words by educators because their purpose is to provide a framework for future vocabulary.

It is typical to start with basic words and expressions you would like to say and consider learning them online, as it is the easiest way to do so typically. You can then use whatever application or website you have chosen to continue learning your basics. The greatest starters are typically greetings, such as yes, no, please, thank you, sorry, and excuse me.

One website particularly useful in learning the basics is FluentU. This is a website that takes real life videos, such as movie trailers, music videos, inspirational talks, and news, and turns all of the content into German language learning lessons. This service is not limited simply to German though. It takes on all of the world languages that most language learning applications usually do.

Study nouns, adjectives, and verbs

Once some basics have been picked up, it becomes very important to supplement your new knowledge with study of basic nouns, adjectives, and verbs. These are the building blocks of language which everything else is founded upon. Once there has been a framework of some fundamental words and expressions established, there can be more and more built upon it. The words best suited for day to day use are best to learn throughout this period. Some examples are listed below:

Woche, week; *Jahr,* year; *Huete,* today; *Morgen,* tomorrow; *Gestern,* yesterday; *Kalender,* calendar; *Sekunde,* second; *Stunde,* hour; *Minute,* minute; *Uhr,* o'clock; *uhr,* clock; *Können,* can; *Benutzen,* use; *Machen,* do; *Gehen,* go; *Kommen,* come; *lachen,* laugh; *Machen,* make; *Sehen,* see; *Weit,* far; *Klein,* small; *Gut,* good; *Schön,* beautiful; *Hässlich,* ugly; *Schwierig,* difficult.

Come to understand the construction of sentences

The next step in the learning of the language is developing skills in regard to sentence structure. It is beneficial to the learner that most will understand the information construed with or without proper sentence structure, but this nevertheless remains one of the most important aspects of learning any language. Compared to English, German has more options and intricacies in the structuring of sentences, some of which will not be listed here:

The sentence 'I am giving the cat a mouse' would, for instance, translate into *'Ich gebe die Mauze zur Katze'* in German. *Katze* would be in the dative mode here, while *Mauze* would be in the accusative. It is sometimes easy to struggle in remembering which prepositions are in the dative or accusative modes, but there is also some good news for those who have difficulty with this: at certain times, such as this one, it is possible to omit the preposition of a sentence altogether and still retain the ability to clearly express the intention of the sentence by use of its word order and proper noun cases.

Without the preposition of *zur (zu+der)*, the sentence could be written as follows:

Ich gebe der Katze die Maus. (*Maus* is accusative, *Katze* is dative.)

Or with a pronoun:

Ich gebe ihr die Maus. (*Maus* is accusative, *Ihr* is dative.)

Ich gebe sie der Katze. (*Katze is* dative, *Sie* is accusative.)

The following rules would be advantageous to keep in mind when positioning a dative and accusative object within a sentence:
> Dative objects forever and always come before accusative objects.
> If the accusative object is a pronoun, however, it will always be placed before any dative objects.

It is always essential to apply these rules with the correct grammatical case endings. It will often help in avoiding misconstrued sentences, such as *Ich gebe der Maus die Katze*. Unless, of course, you really did mean to say that you wanted to give the cat to the mouse.

A few more examples would be:
Gib dem Hasen die Karotte. (Give the bunny the carrot.)
Gib ihr die Karotte. (Give her the carrot.)
Gib es ihr. (Give it to her.)

Starting to learn simple German phrases

Once word order, along with sentence structure, has been learned the next step in the process of learning German would be to start learning basic phrases. Just as was done with simple words, it is useful to start with phrases that the learner would use on a day to day basis.

Watch German language movies

This one is not only useful, but it is also fun. Once a basic understanding of German has been established, one thing to do with movies that you have already seen would be to watch German dubbed versions of them. And, of course, you could also watch new German language movies. It could be helpful to turn on English subtitles while doing this though, as it may prove difficult to follow along with the speech of the films. As you increase and expand on your German speaking skills movie watching can become easier and easier with the passage of time.

As your comprehension level improves, you could even consider watching German language movies with their original German subtitles. This would be a very interactive method to use as it would almost be like seeing German speaking reality unfold with German subtitles included. A great technique for language immersion. Some of the greatest movies Germany has to offer for these purposes are Sonnenallee, Die Legende von Paul und Paula, Der Baader Meinhof Komplex, Die Fette Jahren sind Vorbei, and Joschka und Herr Fischer.

Reading German language news

This one will not only familiarize you with the language of Germany, but also its happenings and culture. This is a particularly great method for use by students who like politics or knowing about world happenings. In addition, it is also great for picking up vocabulary, as new words can always be highlighted and looked up whenever they come up.

Connecting with German language speakers

This one is another extremely important one that has already been touched on in some detail. In addition to the websites previously listed that offer services for doing this, Meetup.com and Craigslist.org are also easy places to meet native German speakers or even other German learners. These websites have active and diligent learners who can be of great help to practice your German speaking skills with. Making connections with these people can also become a great source of accountability and motivation. Similar sites are numerous and can also be used to meet other learners. One of the greatest things about these websites is that you never know who you will make a connection with.

Modernity offers lots of other unusual resources in language learning in addition to the more traditional methods listed above. It can be helpful in learning a new language to weigh as many options as possible because it is never quite clear what route is going to lead to the most rewarding means of educating oneself. Some of these newer methods of foreign language learning are listed below:

Listening to podcasts in German

There are some podcasts out there with the specific purpose of learning the German language. These are especially useful because unlike other language learning resources these can be used anywhere and at any time. One other aspect of this means of learning German to be noted is their entertainment value. Podcasts are always a more immersive and fun experience than reading language learning books. They can also help with pronunciation, as the learner gets German audio, rather than just text.

There are, of course, many other ways to introduce oneself to German language learning, but the ones listed above should provide a decent starting point for any student looking to get his or her feet wet.

Chapter 6:
Learning German in a more formal classroom environment

The German language is one language that increasingly taught at schools all across the world. Most instructional courses on German are within public and private schools and are intended for school aged children and adolescents. There are, however, many German courses intended for the adult looking for further study of the language. In addition, there are many independent tutors available in most cities where German is at all spoken.

Most of these independent courses have enrollment rates ranging from $150-$300 depending on what city they take place in. The hours per week that the classes require are not very extensive or demanding, ranging from 1-10. The overall duration of these courses is, also, not very extensive, ranging from 1-50 weeks usually. The courses are usually for participants aged 18 and up, so it is not typical that the average student will get very many lazy or otherwise bothersome classmates.

The increased opportunity to learn among peers and develop skills with the help of others is probably the best thing that learning German in a classroom setting has to offer. Teachers of these classes usually assign projects to complete with other students in groups. There is opportunity to learn with your peers as well as independently in most classes offered, which gives this method of learning a huge advantage over others which only offer independent or group study. It is like learning a new language itself, sometimes the learner is working with others on developing skills, and most of the time he or she is working independently. The only difference in a classroom setting is that the subject matter is being worked through by a professional instructor, which alleviates so much of the pressure that any given learner has to live with.

These classes, when tailored towards adults, are somewhat like college courses. The workload is typically somewhat robust, though seldom very overwhelming, it is not a very intimate group of classmates, though typically a functional one, and it is usually bereft of the gossip and the bad studentry typical of middle and high schools. It provides a more thorough educational experience mainly because of the fact that students are somewhat obligated to study the material at hand and are more motivated to do so due to their spending of entrance fees. These classes are also beneficial in that students are quizzed and tested here, occurrences that most students would probably not undertake throughout independent study.

Another important element of the classroom learning of German is the ease of the time allotments. Each student agrees to meet at whatever scheduled times there are throughout the week, which makes setting the time aside so much easier. This is also helpful because of the necessity of meeting the schedule. There is added pressure in sticking to a schedule that you as well as others have agreed upon. You are, in a way, made responsible for the successes or the failures of your classmates when you enter one of these classes. One student's absence or poor performance truly can jeopardize the performance of the whole. Foreign language classes are especially beneficial for those who have a hard time keeping and maintaining schedules for this reason.

Another thing preferable about classroom German learning is the motivation an instructor can instill in a student. It becomes so much easier to learn effectively when there is a professional behind you at every step of the process. It gives a learner so much assurance to know that they are relatively safe from any misinformation or bad advice. At the same time, it increases accountability for the learner. He or she becomes responsible for exam scores and homework completion, which in a way enumerates the comprehensive input that the learner is exposed to.

Many German courses independent of formal educational institutions tend to be very student oriented with great student to instructor ratios. The small class sizes tend to make learning much easier and more enjoyable for the average student. It is not uncommon for the instructors of these classes to be able to give all the students one on one attention every day of study.

Conclusion

Congratulations on making it to the end of *Learning German*. Let us hope you have found this book to be both informative and helpful. Let us also hope that all the objectives mentioned in the introduction have met your standards. Now that you have finished this book, it would be useful to apply the skills learned here to any other further practice of the language in the future. There are, as has been mentioned before, many other learning resources out there on this subject available for download or physical purchase.

The next step in your education would be to utilize these resources and find which ones work and don't work for you. The names of multiple websites and apps, most of them free, have been mentioned within this book and there are also many paper materials on the markets useful in learning German.

It is a notable fact that complex tasks have a much higher completion rate when compartmentalized into more digestible parts than when they are left as the big hydras that they start out as. This is useful to know in learning German, and with this information the contents of this book can be made more accessible and serve greater utility to the reader.

Once the initial stages of learning the German language listed in this book have been surpassed, it at once becomes much easier to continue learning. Learning at this stage also becomes more effective and vocabulary and grammar skills work on top of one another to make fluency a reality, eventually and with practice. As in the case of developing any other skill, the learning of German takes, above all, practice and persistence. It is ultimately those who stick with the study the longest and the hardest who get the best results in the end.

And again, if this book proved to be at all helpful or useful to you, a review on Amazon would be greatly appreciated.

www.ingramcontent.com/pod-product-compliance
Lightning Source LLC
Chambersburg PA
CBHW050204130526
44591CB00034B/2143